THE ULTIMATE
SEATTLE MARINERS
TRIVIA BOOK

A Collection of Amazing Trivia Quizzes
and Fun Facts for Die-Hard Mariners Fans!

Ray Walker

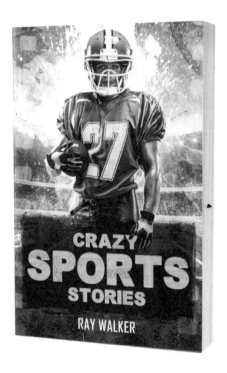

CONTENTS

INTRODUCTION

The Seattle Mariners were established in 1977 as an MLB expansion team. Since their establishment, they have consistently proven themselves to be a team who fights hard and is a force to be reckoned with in the MLB.

Although the Seattle Mariners have not yet won a World Series title, or an American League pennant, they have won three West division titles and one Wild Card berth. They are often a threat in the American League West Division, having last won it in 2001.

The Mariners currently call T-Mobile Park home, which opened in 1999. They play in one of the most difficult divisions in baseball, the American League West, alongside the Oakland A's, Los Angeles Angels, Texas Rangers, and Houston Astros.

The thing about baseball is that it is a lot like life. There are good times and bad times, good days and bad days, but you have to do your absolute best to never give up. The Seattle Mariners have proven that they refuse to give up, and that they will do anything they need to do in order to bring a championship to the state of Washington.

Winning is more than possible when you have a storied past like the Seattle Mariners. They have so much captivating history and so many undeniable player legacies to be profoundly proud of. Especially when you think about the player numbers already retired by the franchise: Ken Griffey Jr. and Edgar Martinez—in addition to the league's retiring legendary Jackie Robinson's uniform number.

With such a storied team past, that goes back generations and up until the 2020 season, you're probably already very knowledgeable as the die-hard M's fan that you are. Let's test that knowledge to see if you truly are the world's biggest Mariners fan.

CHAPTER 1:

ORIGINS & HISTORY

QUIZ TIME!

1. Which of the following team names did the Mariners franchise once go by?

    a. Seattle Mavericks

    b. Seattle Expos

    c. Seattle Sun Devils

    d. They have always been the Mariners.

2. In what year was the Seattle Mariners franchise established?

    a. 1957

    b. 1967

    c. 1977

    d. 1987

3. The Seattle Mariners' current home stadium is T-Mobile Park.

    a. True

    b. False

4. Which division do the Seattle Mariners play in currently?

   a. American League Central

   b. American League West

   c. National League Central

   d. National League West

5. The Seattle Mariners have never won a Wild Card berth.

   a. True

   b. False

6. How many American League pennants has the Seattle Mariners franchise won?

   a. 0

   b. 1

   c. 2

   d. 3

7. As of the end of the 2020 season, the Seattle Mariners hold the longest playoff drought in all of the four major North American professional sports.

   a. True

   b. False

8. Who is the winningest manager in Seattle Mariners history?

   a. Dick Williams

   b. Mike Hargrove

   c. Bob Melvin

   d. Lou Piniella

9. What is the name of the Seattle Mariners' Triple-A team, and where are they located?

   a. Nashville Sounds
   b. Tacoma Rainiers
   c. Omaha Storm Chasers
   d. Jacksonville Jumbo Shrimp

10. Who was the first manager of the Mariners franchise?

   a. Chuck Cottier
   b. Rene Lachemann
   c. Darrell Johnson
   d. Maury Wills

11. The Seattle Mariners were members of the National League West Division from 1977 to 1993.

   a. True
   b. False

12. What is the name of the Seattle Mariners' current Spring Training home stadium?

   a. Hohokam Stadium
   b. Peoria Sports Complex
   c. Tempe Diablo Stadium
   d. Salt River Fields at Talking Stick

13. How many appearances has the Seattle Mariners franchise made in the MLB playoffs?

   a. 1
   b. 2
   c. 3
   d. 4

14. How many World Series titles have the Seattle Mariners won?

    a. 0
    b. 1
    c. 2
    d. 3

15. The Seattle Mariners' current manager is Scott Servais.

    a. True
    b. False

16. Which stadium was the first home of the Seattle Mariners franchise?

    a. Sportsman's Park
    b. T-Mobile Park
    c. Kingdome
    d. Safeco Field

17. Who is the current general manager of the Seattle Mariners?

    a. Mike Rizzo
    b. Mike Elias
    c. David Forst
    d. Jerry Dipoto

18. How many American League West division titles have the Seattle Mariners won?

    a. 1
    b. 2
    c. 3
    d. 4

19. The "Mariners" name was inspired by the prominence of marine culture in the city of Seattle.

    a. True
    b. False

20. The Seattle Mariners are currently owned by the Baseball Club of Seattle represented by CEO John Stanton and Nintendo of America.

    a. True
    b. False

QUIZ ANSWERS

1. D – They have always been the Mariners.

2. C – 1977

3. A – True

4. B – American League West

5. B – False (They won one berth in 2000.)

6. A – 0

7. A – True

8. D – Lou Piniella

9. B – Tacoma Rainiers

10. C – Darrell Johnson

11. B – False

12. B – Peoria Sports Complex

13. D – 4

14. A – 0

15. A – True

16. C – Kingdome

17. D – Jerry Dipoto

18. C – 3

19. A – True

20. A – True

DID YOU KNOW?

1. The Seattle Mariners franchise has had 20 managers so far, which include: Darrell Johnson, Maury Wills, Rene Lachemann, Del Crandall, Chuck Cottier, Marty Martinez, Dick Williams, Jim Snyder, Jim Lefebvre, Bill Plummer, Lou Piniella, Bob Melvin, Mike Hargrove, John McLaren, Jim Riggleman, Don Wakamatsu, Daren Brown, Eric Wedge, Lloyd McClendon, and Scott Servais.

2. The Seattle Mariners' current manager is Scott Servais, who previously played in the MLB as a catcher for 11 seasons. He played for the Houston Astros, Chicago Cubs, San Francisco Giants, and Colorado Rockies. He was previously the assistant general manager for the Los Angeles Angels of Anaheim and director of player development for the Texas Rangers. He has been the Mariners' manager since 2016.

3. Lou Piniella is the Seattle Mariners' all-time winningest manager with a record of 840-711 (.542). He managed the Seattle Mariners from 1993 to 2002.

4. John Stanton is the current CEO of the Seattle Mariners. He is the chairman of the board of Trilogy International Partners and founder of several wireless companies.

5. The Seattle Mariners franchise has hosted two MLB All-Star Games so far: the 1979 game was held at the Kingdome, and the 2001 game was held at Safeco Field.

6. The Seattle Mariners have had six no-hitters thrown in franchise history. The first occurred in 1990, thrown by Randy Johnson, and the latest occurred in 2018, thrown by James Paxton. There has been one perfect game in Seattle Mariners history so far, which was thrown by Felix Hernandez in 2012.

7. The Mariners set the American League record for most wins in a single season by winning 116 games in 2001. This milestone tied them with the 1906 Chicago Cubs for the MLB record of most single-season wins.

8. The Seattle Mariners' Double-A team is the Arkansas Travelers. High-A is the Everett AquaSox. Low-A is the Modesto Nuts.

9. The Seattle Mariners' current mascot is named Mariner Moose.

10. In 2001, the Seattle Mariners set an American League record for most wins in a single season with 116.

CHAPTER 2:

JERSEYS & NUMBERS

QUIZ TIME!

1. The Seattle Mariners' original team colors were blue and gold.

   a. True
   b. False

2. What are the Seattle Mariners' current official team colors?

   a. Royal blue, metallic silver, northwest green, and gray
   b. Navy blue, metallic silver, royal blue, and cream
   c. Navy blue, metallic silver, northwest green, royal blue, yellow, and cream
   d. Royal blue, yellow, cream, and metallic silver

3. From 1977 to 1980, the Seattle Mariners wore baby blue road uniforms.

   a. True
   b. False

4. Which of the following numbers in NOT retired by the Seattle Mariners?

   a. 11
   b. 24
   c. 35
   d. 42

5. What uniform number does Kyle Seager currently wear as a member of the Seattle Mariners?

   a. 5
   b. 15
   c. 25
   d. 55

6. What uniform number did Ken Griffey Jr. wear during his time with the Seattle Mariners?

   a. 2
   b. 4
   c. 24
   d. 42

7. Edgar Martinez wore the uniform number 11 during his time with the Seattle Mariners.

   a. True
   b. False

8. James Jones, Daniel Robertson, and which other player are the only three Seattle Mariners players to have ever worn the uniform number 99 in franchise history?

   a. Tyler Olson
   b. Matt Festa

c. Taijuan Walker

d. Jean Machi

9. Who is the only Seattle Mariners player to have ever worn the uniform number 0?

a. Jeffrey Leonard

b. Jarrod Dyson

c. Eric Byrnes

d. Mallex Smith

10. No Seattle Mariners player has ever worn the uniform number 00.

a. True

b. False

11. What uniform number did Ichiro Suzuki wear as a member of the Seattle Mariners?

a. 21

b. 31

c. 41

d. 51

12. What uniform number did Alex Rodriguez wear as a member of the Seattle Mariners?

a. 3

b. 13

c. 33

d. Both A and B

13. Both Felix Hernandez and Randy Johnson wore the uniform numbers 34 and 59 during their time with the Seattle Mariners.

    a. True

    b. False

14. What uniform number did Jamie Moyer wear as a member of the Seattle Mariners?

    a. 20

    b. 30

    c. 40

    d. 50

15. What uniform number did Robinson Cano wear as a member of the Seattle Mariners?

    a. 14

    b. 22

    c. 24

    d. Both B and C

16. What uniform number did Jay Buhner wear as a member of the Seattle Mariners?

    a. 11

    b. 19

    c. 43

    d. Both B and C

17. During his time with the Seattle Mariners, which uniform number did Alvin Davis wear?

    a. 1

    b. 11

c. 21

d. 31

18. What uniform number did Mark Langston wear with the Seattle Mariners?

    a. 6

    b. 12

    c. 18

    d. 22

19. What uniform number did Freddy Garcia wear as a member of the Seattle Mariners?

    a. 3

    b. 4

    c. 34

    d. 43

20. Harold Reynolds wore the uniform numbers 4, 18, 19, and 24 during his time with the Seattle Mariners.

    a. True

    b. False

QUIZ ANSWERS

1. A – True
2. C – Navy blue, metallic silver, northwest green, royal blue, yellow, and cream
3. A – True
4. C – 35
5. B – 15
6. C – 24
7. A – True
8. C – Taijuan Walker
9. D – Mallex Smith
10. B – False (Jeffrey Leonard wore number 00 from 1989 to 1990.)
11. D – 51
12. A – 3
13. A – True
14. D – 50
15. B – 22
16. D – Both B and C
17. C – 21
18. B – 12
19. C – 34
20. A – True

DID YOU KNOW?

1. The Seattle Mariners have retired three uniform numbers overall in franchise history: Edgar Martinez (number 11), Ken Griffey Jr. (number 21), and Jackie Robinson (number 42).

2. Adrian Beltre wore the uniform numbers 5 and 29 during his time with the Seattle Mariners.

3. Bret Boone wore the uniform numbers 5 and 29 during his time with the Seattle Mariners.

4. During his time with the Seattle Mariners, Mike Cameron wore the uniform number 44.

5. During his time with the Seattle Mariners, Mike Moore wore the uniform number 25.

6. During his time with the Seattle Mariners, John Olreud wore the uniform number 5.

7. Jackie Robinson's number 42 is retired by the Seattle Mariners as well as the MLB as a whole. No Mariners or MLB player will ever wear number 42 again. The Yankees' Mariano Rivera was the final player to wear it.

8. During his time with the Seattle Mariners, Nelson Cruz wore the uniform number 23.

9. During his time with the Seattle Mariners, Raúl Ibañez wore the uniform numbers 5, 23, 26, 28, and 38.

10. During his time with the Seattle Mariners, Jim Beattie wore the uniform number 45.

CHAPTER 3:

AMERICA'S PASTIME

QUIZ TIME!

1. How many teams play in Major League Baseball?

    a. 15
    b. 20
    c. 30
    d. 33

2. Major League Baseball was founded in 1903.

    a. True
    b. False

3. Who is the current commissioner of Major League Baseball?

    a. Bart Giamatti
    b. Fay Vincent
    c. Bud Selig
    d. Rob Manfred

4. What year was the National League founded?

a. 1870

b. 1876

c. 1903

d. 1911

5. What year was the American League founded?

a. 1888

b. 1901

c. 1903

d. 1918

6. Major League Baseball is the second wealthiest professional sports league. Which league is the wealthiest?

a. NBA

b. NHL

c. NFL

d. MLS

7. The Major League Baseball headquarters is located in New York City.

a. True

b. False

8. How many games does each Major League Baseball team play per season?

a. 92

b. 122

c. 162

d. 192

9. In which two US states is Major League Baseball's Spring Training held?

    a. California and Florida
    b. Arizona and Florida
    c. Arizona and California
    d. California and Arkansas

10. How many stitches does a baseball used in Major League games have?

    a. 98
    b. 100
    c. 108
    d. 110

11. Where is the National Baseball Hall of Fame located?

    a. Denver, Colorado
    b. Phoenix, Arizona
    c. Los Angeles, California
    d. Cooperstown, New York

12. All 30 Major League Baseball teams are located in the United States.

    a. True
    b. False

13. Which current Major League Baseball stadium is the oldest stadium still in use?

    a. Angel Stadium
    b. Dodger Stadium
    c. Fenway Park
    d. Wrigley Field

14. Major League Baseball has the highest attendance of any sports league in the world.

    a. True
    b. False

15. Fill in the blank: Seventh Inning _____

    a. Jog
    b. Song
    c. Shake
    d. Stretch

16. William Howard Taft was the first United States president to throw out the ceremonial first pitch at a Major League Baseball game.

    a. True
    b. False

17. It is a Major League Baseball rule that all umpires must wear which color underwear in case they rip their pants?

    a. Tan
    b. Gray
    c. White
    d. Black

18. What year did the first Major League Baseball World Series take place?

    a. 1903
    b. 1905
    c. 1915
    d. 1920

19. Former Major League Baseball Commissioner Bart Giamatti is the father of actor Paul Giamatti.

    a. True
    b. False

20. The song traditionally played in the middle of the 7th inning at Major League Baseball games is "Take Me Out to the Ballpark."

    a. True
    b. False

QUIZ ANSWERS

1. C – 30

2. A – True

3. D – Rob Manfred

4. B – 1876

5. B – 1901

6. C – NFL

7. A – True

8. C – 162

9. B – Arizona and Florida

10. C – 108

11. D – Cooperstown, New York

12. B – False (Only 29 teams are in the US; the Toronto Blue Jays are located in Canada.)

13. C – Fenway Park

14. A – True

15. D – Stretch

16. A – True

17. D – Black

18. A – 1903

19. A – True

20. B – False (The song is called "Take Me Out to the Ball Game.")

DID YOU KNOW?

1. The average lifespan of a baseball in a Major League game is 5-7 pitches. This means approximately 5-6 dozen baseballs are used in every game.

2. The Boston Americans won the very first World Series. They defeated the Pittsburgh Pirates in eight games. Today, the most games a World Series can go is seven.

3. As of the end of the 2020 season, the New York Yankees currently hold the most World Series titles in Major League Baseball, with 27.

4. Hot dogs are the most popular food item sold at Major League Baseball ballparks. Over 21 million hot dogs were sold at MLB stadiums in 2014.

5. The longest Major League game on record occurred on May 9, 1984, between the Chicago White Sox and Milwaukee Brewers. The game lasted 8 hours, 6 minutes. The most innings played in a Major League game were 26 innings on May 1, 1920. The game was between the Brooklyn Dodgers and Boston Braves.

6. The mound to home plate distance at Major League Baseball ballparks is 60 feet, 6 inches.

7. Before they can be used in a Major League game, each baseball is rubbed with a special mud to improve grip

and reduce luster. This special mud comes from a specific, secret location in the state of New Jersey.

8. The fastest Major League game on record took place on September 28, 1919, between the New York Giants and Philadelphia Phillies, and lasted only 51 minutes. An average MLB game is three hours.

9. The American League uses a designated hitter. A DH only hits and does not play in the field. In the National League, the pitcher hits instead of using a designated hitter. If an interleague game is being played, whether a DH is used or not is determined by which team is the home team. If the home team is from the American League, each team will use a DH. If the home team is from the National League, each team's pitcher will hit.

10. The distance between each of the four bases in Major League Baseball is 90 feet.

CHAPTER 4:

CATCHY NICKNAMES

QUIZ TIME!

1. What nickname does Ken Griffey Jr. go by?

    a. "Junior"

    b. "The Kid"

    c. "The Natural"

    d. All of the above

2. Edgar Martinez goes by the nicknames "Gar" and "Papi."

    a. True

    b. False

3. Which of the following is a common nickname for the Seattle Mariners as a team?

    a. The Sea Men

    b. The M's

    c. The Mar's

    d. The 'Ners

4. What nickname does Felix Hernandez go by?

a. "Mr. Felix"

b. "Prince Felix"

c. "King Felix"

d. "Flamin' Felix"

5. What nickname does Randy Johnson go by?

a. "Big Boy"

b. "Big Rand"

c. "Big Hurt"

d. "Big Unit"

6. Which nickname does Alex Rodriguez go by?

a. "Runnin' Rodriguez"

b. "A-Rod"

c. "Hot Rod"

d. "Al-Rod"

7. Ichiro Suzuki goes by the nicknames "Ichi" and "Wizard."

a. True

b. False

8. What nickname does Jay Buhner go by?

a. "Toe"

b. "Finger"

c. "Bone"

d. "Brain"

9. What nickname does Freddy Garcia go by?

a. "The Chief"

b. "The Rock"

c. "The King"

d. Both A and B

10. What nickname does Mike Cameron go by?

a. "C-Man"

b. "Cammy"

c. "Mike-Ron"

d. "Cam Cam"

11. What nickname does Nelson Cruz go by?

a. "Cruzin"

b. "Slamstick"

c. "Boomstick"

d. "Sonny"

12. Adrian Beltre goes by the nickname "El Koja."

a. True

b. False

13. Which nickname does Chris Davis go by?

a. "Coca Cola"

b. "Crush"

c. "Dr. Davis"

d. "Seven Up"

14. What nickname does Omar Vizquel go by?

a. "Little V"

b. "Big V"

c. "Little O"

d. "Big O"

15. Robinson Cano goes by the simple nickname "Robbie."

    a. True

    b. False

16. "Goose" is a nickname. What is Goose Gossage's real first name?

    a. Zachary

    b. Harold

    c. James

    d. Richard

17. Willie Bloomquist goes by the nickname "Spork."

    a. True

    b. False

18. "J.J." is a nickname. What is J.J. Putz's full name?

    a. Jason Joseph Putz

    b. Joseph Jason Putz

    c. Jacob James Putz

    d. James Jacob Putz

19. What was Dave Henderson's nickname?

    a. "Hends"

    b. "Hendy"

    c. "Hendu"

    d. "Hendo"

20. "Bud" is a nickname. Bud Black's full name is Harry Ralston Black.

    a. True

    b. False

QUIZ ANSWERS

1. D – All of the above

2. A – True

3. B – The M's

4. C – "King Felix"

5. D – "Big Unit"

6. B – "A-Rod"

7. A – True

8. C – "Bone"

9. D – Both A and B

10. B – "Cammy"

11. C – "Boomstick"

12. A – True

13. B – "Crush"

14. C – "Little O"

15. A – True

16. D – Richard

17. A – True

18. B – Joseph Jason Putz

19. C – "Hendu"

20. A – True

DID YOU KNOW?

1. Kevin Mitchell goes by the nicknames "World," "Mitchell Monster," "Boogie Bear," and "Tatonka."

2. Former Mariners manager Lou Piniella goes by the nickname "Sweet Lou."

3. James Paxton was born in Canada and goes by the nickname "The Big Maple."

4. Former Mariners manager Bob Melvin goes by the nickname "BoMel."

5. Dan Wilson goes by the nickname "Willie."

6. Rickey Henderson goes by the nickname "Man of Steal."

7. Tom Paciorek goes by the nickname "Wimpy."

8. Al Cowens went by the nickname "A.C."

9. "Tino" is a nickname. Tino Martinez's full name is Constantino Martinez. Another nickname of his includes "Bamtino."

10. Mike Morse goes by the nickname "The Beast."

CHAPTER 5:

JUNIOR

QUIZ TIME!

1. What is Ken Griffey Jr.'s full name?

    a. James Kenneth Griffey Jr.

    b. Kenneth James Griffey Jr.

    c. Kenneth George Griffey Jr

    d. George Kenneth Griffey Jr.

2. Ken Griffey Jr. played his entire 22-season MLB career with the Seattle Mariners.

    a. True

    b. False

3. Where was Ken Griffey Jr. born?

    a. Seattle, Washington

    b. Cincinnati, Ohio

    c. Donora, Pennsylvania

    d. Philadelphia, Pennsylvania

4. When was Ken Griffey Jr. born?

a. November 29, 1969

b. November 29, 1972

c. October 29, 1969

d. October 29, 1972

5. Ken Griffey Jr.'s dad, Ken Griffey Sr., played for the Seattle Mariners alongside his son during the 1990 and 1991 seasons.

a. True

b. False

6. How many MLB All-Star Games was Ken Griffey Jr. named to during his MLB career?

a. 8

b. 10

c. 13

d. 15

7. Ken Griffey Jr. was named the All-Star Game MVP in which year?

a. 1990

b. 1991

c. 1992

d. 1993

8. Ken Griffey Jr. was named the 1989 American League Rookie of the Year.

a. True

b. False

9. What year was Ken Griffey Jr. inducted into the National Baseball Hall of Fame with 99.3% of the vote?

    a. 2016
    b. 2017
    c. 2018
    d. 2019

10. How many Gold Glove Awards did Ken Griffey Jr. win during his MLB career?

    a. 7
    b. 8
    c. 9
    d. 10

11. How many Silver Slugger Awards did Ken Griffey Jr. win during his MLB career?

    a. 5
    b. 7
    c. 9
    d. 10

12. Ken Griffey Jr. was named the 1997 Major League Player of the Year.

    a. True
    b. False

13. How many times was Ken Griffey Jr. named the American League MVP during his MLB career?

    a. 1
    b. 2

c. 3

d. 4

14. Ken Griffey Jr.'s uniform number 24 was the first uniform number to be retired by the Seattle Mariners.

    a. True

    b. False

15. How many times did Ken Griffey Jr. win the MLB Home Run Derby?

    a. 1

    b. 2

    c. 3

    d. 4

16. How many total home runs did Ken Griffey Jr. hit during his MLB career?

    a. 620

    b. 630

    c. 640

    d. 650

17. Ken Griffey Jr.'s career batting average is .284.

    a. True

    b. False

18. How many hits did Ken Griffey Jr. make during his MLB career?

    a. 2,761

    b. 2,771

c. 2,781

d. 2,791

19. How many RBIs did Ken Griffey Jr. collect during his MLB career?

    a. 1,536

    b. 1,636

    c. 1,736

    d. 1,836

20. Ken Griffey Jr. is one of 29 players in league history to have appeared in MLB games in four different decades.

    a. True

    b. False

QUIZ ANSWERS

1. D – George Kenneth Griffey Jr.

2. B – False (He played for the Mariners, Reds, and White Sox.)

3. C – Donora, Pennsylvania

4. A – November 29, 1969

5. A – True

6. C – 13

7. C – 1992

8. B – False (Gregg Olson was 1989 AL Rookie of the Year; Junior came in 3rd place.)

9. A – 2016

10. D – 10

11. B – 7

12. A – True

13. A – 1 (1997)

14. A – True

15. C – 3 (1994, 1998, 1999)

16. B – 630

17. A – True

18. C – 2,781

19. D – 1,836

20. A – True

DID YOU KNOW?

1. On August 6, 2016, Ken Griffey Jr.'s uniform number 24 became the first retired by the Mariners. Number 24 is also retired throughout the Mariners' entire Minor League system.

2. Ken Griffey Jr.'s son Trey played in the NFL as a wide receiver for the Indianapolis Colts, Miami Dolphins, and Pittsburgh Steelers.

3. After his retirement from baseball, Ken Griffey Jr. joined the Mariners' front office as a special consultant.

4. Ken Griffey Jr. is a member of both the Mariners' and the Reds' Halls of Fame.

5. Ken Griffey Jr. was on the cover of the video game *MLB The Show* 2017.

6. The Griffey family joined as a minority owner of the Seattle Sounders FC on November 17, 2020.

7. Ken Griffey Jr. and Chipper Jones are the only two National Baseball Hall of Fame inductees who were also chosen 1st overall in an MLB Draft.

8. A flag with Ken Griffey Jr.'s uniform number 24 on it was flown from Seattle's Space Needle following the announcement of his induction into the National Baseball Hall of Fame.

9. Ken Griffey Jr. was elected to the National Baseball Hall of Fame with 99.32% of the vote. This broke the record previously held by Tom Seaver at 98.84%, which was set in 1992.

10. Ken Griffey Jr. starred in the famous baseball episode of *The Simpsons* entitled "Homer and the Bat" alongside fellow MLB stars including: Roger Clemens, Wade Boggs, Steve Sax, Ozzie Smith, José Canseco, Don Mattingly, Darryl Strawberry, and Mike Scioscia.

CHAPTER 6:

STATISTICALLY SPEAKING

QUIZ TIME!

1. Ken Griffey Jr. currently holds the Seattle Mariners franchise record for the most home runs. How many home runs did he hit over the course of his MLB career?

   a. 407
   b. 417
   c. 427
   d. 437

2. Pitcher Felix Hernandez has the most wins in Seattle Mariners franchise history, with 169.

   a. True
   b. False

3. Which pitcher holds the Seattle Mariners record for most career shutouts thrown, with 19?

   a. Felix Hernandez
   b. Mark Langston
   c. Mike Moore

d. Randy Johnson

4. Which Seattle Mariners batter currently holds the single-season record for strikeouts, with 176?

   a. Nelson Cruz
   b. Jim Presley
   c. Mike Cameron
   d. Jay Buhner

5. How many strikeouts does Felix Hernandez have to hold the title of most in Seattle Mariners franchise history?

   a. 2,494
   b. 2,504
   c. 2,514
   d. 2,524

6. Who has the most stolen bases in Seattle Mariners franchise history, with 438?

   a. Julio Cruz
   b. Ichiro Suzuki
   c. Harold Reynolds
   d. Ken Griffey Jr.

7. Kazuhiro Sasaki holds the record for most saves in Seattle Mariners history, with 129.

   a. True
   b. False

8. Ken Griffey Jr. and Ichiro Suzuki are tied for the Seattle Mariners record for being intentionally walked, with how many?

a. 152

b. 162

c. 172

d. 182

9. Which player holds the Seattle Mariners franchise record for home runs in a single season, with 56?

a. Jay Buhner

b. Ken Griffey Jr.

c. Nelson Cruz

d. Alex Rodriguez

10. Which batter holds the single-season Seattle Mariners record for hits, with 262?

a. Alex Rodriguez

b. Ken Griffey Jr.

c. Ichiro Suzuki

d. Edgar Martinez

11. Who holds the single-season Seattle Mariners record for double plays grounded into, with 29?

a. Robinson Cano

b. Tino Martinez

c. Bruce Bochte

d. Jim Presley

12. Edgar Martinez holds the record for the most sacrifice flies in Seattle Mariners all-time franchise history, with 77.

a. True

b. False

13. Felix Hernandez threw the highest number of wild pitches in Seattle Mariners franchise history, with how many?

    a. 42
    b. 43
    c. 66
    d. 156

14. Which player holds the single-season Seattle Mariners record for the most triples, with 12?

    a. Ichiro Suzuki
    b. Harold Reynolds
    c. Ruppert Jones
    d. Phil Bradley

15. Which hitter has the most walks in Seattle Mariners franchise history, with 1,283?

    a. Jay Buhner
    b. Alvin Davis
    c. Edgar Martinez
    d. Ken Griffey Jr.

16. Which Seattle Mariners hitter holds the all-time franchise record for best overall batting average at .321?

    a. Ken Griffey Jr.
    b. Ichiro Suzuki
    c. Edgar Martinez
    d. Alex Rodriguez

17. Edgar Martinez holds the Seattle Mariners record for most runs scored, with 1,219.

    a. True
    b. False

18. Edgar Martinez has the most plate appearances all time in Mariners franchise history, with how many?

    a. 8,474
    b. 8,574
    c. 8,674
    d. 8,774

19. Which pitcher holds the Seattle Mariners franchise record for most saves in a single season, with 57?

    a. Kazuhiro Sasaki
    b. J.J. Putz
    c. Fernando Rodney
    d. Edwin Diaz

20. Felix Hernandez holds the Mariners franchise record for most losses, with 136.

    a. True
    b. False

QUIZ ANSWERS

1. B – 417

2. A – True

3. D – Randy Johnson

4. C – Mike Cameron (2002)

5. D – 2,524

6. B – Ichiro Suzuki

7. A – True

8. C – 172

9. B – Ken Griffey Jr. (For 1997 and 1998—He holds the top five spots of this Mariners record.)

10. C – Ichiro Suzuki (2004)

11. D – Jim Presley (1985)

12. A – True

13. D – 156

14. A – Ichiro Suzuki (2005)

15. C – Edgar Martinez

16. B – Ichiro Suzuki

17. A – True

18. C – 8,674

19. D – Edwin Diaz (2018)

20. A – True

DID YOU KNOW?

1. Felix Hernandez threw the most innings in Seattle Mariners franchise history, with 2,729.02 total. Coming in second is Jamie Moyer who threw 2,093.0 innings total.

2. Ichiro Suzuki had the best single-season batting average in Seattle Mariners franchise history at .372 in 2004. Coming in second is Alex Rodriguez whose batting average was .258 in 1996.

3. Henry Cotto holds the Seattle Mariners franchise record for stolen base percentage, with 84.30% accuracy. Ichiro Suzuki holds the Seattle Mariners franchise record for stolen bases, with 438. Harold Reynolds holds the Seattle Mariners franchise record for the most times caught stealing at 120.

4. Edgar Martinez has the most extra-base hits in Seattle Mariners franchise history, with 838. Second on the list is Ken Griffey Jr. with 788.

5. Ken Phelps holds the Seattle Mariners franchise record for at-bats per home run at 13.3. Essentially, what this means is that, on average, Phelps hit a home run about every 13-14 at-bats.

6. Randy Johnson holds the Seattle Mariners franchise record for strikeouts per nine innings pitched, at 10.585. Essentially, what this means is that, during his time with

the Mariners, the "Big Unit" recorded about 10-11 strikeouts in every nine innings that he pitched.

7. Jose Guillen holds the single-season Seattle Mariners record for the most hit by pitches with 29 in 2007. Randy Johnson holds the single-season Seattle Mariners record for most batters hit with 18 in 1992.

8. Edgar Martinez holds the Seattle Mariners franchise record for career doubles hit, with 514. Second on the list is Ken Griffey Jr. with 341.

9. Jamie Moyer holds the Seattle Mariners single-season record for wins with 21 in 2003. Mike Moore (1987) and Matt Young (1985) are tied for the Seattle Mariners single-season record for most losses, with 19 each.

10. Kazuhiro Sasaki holds the Seattle Mariners franchise record for most saves, with 129.

CHAPTER 7:

THE TRADE MARKET

QUIZ TIME!

1. On May 25, 1989, the Seattle Mariners traded Mark Langston and a player to be named later (Mike Campbell) to which team for Randy Johnson, Gene Harris, and Brian Holman?

   a. New York Yankees
   b. California Angels
   c. Montreal Expos
   d. Houston Astros

2. On February 10, 2000, the Seattle Mariners traded Ken Griffey Jr. to which team for Mike Cameron, Antonio Perez, Brett Tomko, and Jake Meyer?

   a. Boston Red Sox
   b. Chicago Cubs
   c. Chicago White Sox
   d. Cincinnati Reds

3. The Seattle Mariners have made seven trades with the Arizona Diamondbacks as of the end of the 2020 season.

   a. True

   b. False

4. On February 8, 2008, which team traded Erik Bedard to the Seattle Mariners for Adam Jones, George Sherrill, Chris Tillman, Kam Mickolio, and Tony Butler?

   a. Arizona Diamondbacks

   b. Tampa Bay Rays

   c. Baltimore Orioles

   d. Pittsburgh Pirates

5. The Seattle Mariners have made seven trades with the Colorado Rockies all time.

   a. True

   b. False

6. On July 21, 1988, the Seattle Mariners traded Ken Phelps to the New York Yankees for a player to be named later (Troy Evers), Rick Balabon, and who?

   a. Steve Balboni

   b. Jay Buhner

   c. Jim Beattie

   d. Gaylord Perry

7. On July 30, 1996, the Seattle Mariners traded Darren Bragg to which team for Jamie Moyer?

   a. Chicago Cubs

   b. St. Louis Cardinals

c. Philadelphia Phillies

d. Boston Red Sox

8. On December 3, 2018, the Seattle Mariners traded Robinson Cano, Edwin Diaz, and cash considerations to which team for Jay Bruce, Justin Dunn, Anthony Swarzak, Gerson Bautista, and Jarred Kelenic?

a. New York Yankees

b. New York Mets

c. Chicago White Sox

d. Detroit Tigers

9. On July 21, 2017, the Seattle Mariners traded Tyler O'Neill to the St. Louis Cardinals for who?

a. Taijuan Walker

b. Justus Sheffield

c. Marco Gonzales

d. Justin Dunn

10. As of the 2020 season, the Seattle Mariners have made only eight trades with the Florida/Miami Marlins all time.

a. True

b. False

11. On August 27, 2020, the Seattle Mariners traded Taijuan Walker to which team for a player to be named later (Alberto Rodriguez)?

a. Oakland A's

b. Arizona Diamondbacks

c. San Diego Padres

d. Toronto Blue Jays

12. As of the end of 2020, the Seattle Mariners have made only 13 trades with the Oakland A's all time.

    a. True
    b. False

13. How many trades have the Seattle Mariners made with the Los Angeles Angels as of the end of the 2020 season?

    a. 4
    b. 6
    c. 9
    d. 13

14. The Seattle Mariners have made only eight trades with the Detroit Tigers as of the end of the 2020 season.

    a. True
    b. False

15. On December 8, 1978, the Seattle Mariners traded Craig Reynolds to the Houston Astros for which player?

    a. Leon Roberts
    b. Bob Stinson
    c. Larry Milbourne
    d. Floyd Bannister

16. On November 2, 1993, the Seattle Mariners traded Bret Boone and Erik Hanson to which team for Dan Wilson and Bobby Ayala?

    a. San Diego Padres
    b. Minnesota Twins
    c. Cincinnati Reds
    d. Atlanta Braves

17. On January 8, 2004, the Seattle Mariners traded which player to the Detroit Tigers for Ramon Santiago and Juan Gonzalez?

    a. Hiram Bocachica

    b. Freddy Garcia

    c. Carlos Guillen

    d. Ruben Sierra

18. On December 16, 2001, the Seattle Mariners traded Brian Fuentes, Jose Paniagua, and Denny Stark to which team for Jeff Cirillo?

    a. St. Louis Cardinals

    b. Colorado Rockies

    c. Oakland A's

    d. Los Angeles Angels

19. On July 26, 2006, the Seattle Mariners traded Shin-Soo Choo and a player to be named later (Shawn Nottingham) to which team for Ben Broussard and cash considerations?

    a. Kansas City Royals

    b. Cincinnati Reds

    c. Cleveland Indians

    d. Texas Rangers

20. The Seattle Mariners have made five trades with the Tampa Bay Rays/Devil Rays all time.

    a. True

    b. False

QUIZ ANSWERS

1. C – Montreal Expos

2. D – Cincinnati Reds

3. A – True

4. C – Baltimore Orioles

5. A – True

6. B – Jay Buhner

7. D – Boston Red Sox

8. B – New York Mets

9. C – Marco Gonzales

10. A – True

11. D – Toronto Blue Jays

12. A – True

13. A – 4

14. B – False (The Mariners and Tigers made 18 trades all time.)

15. D – Floyd Bannister

16. C – Cincinnati Reds

17. C – Carlos Guillen

18. B – Colorado Rockies

19. C – Cleveland Indians

20. B – False (The Mariners and Rays/Devil Rays have made 18 trades.)

DID YOU KNOW?

1. On July 31, 1998, the Seattle Mariners traded Randy Johnson to the Houston Astros for Freddy Garcia, Carlos Guillen, and a player to be named later (John Halama).

2. On December 2, 2015, the Baltimore Orioles traded Steve Clevenger to the Seattle Mariners for Mark Trumbo and C.J. Riefenhauser.

3. On December 10, 1993, the Seattle Mariners traded Mike Hampton and Mike Felder to the Houston Astros for Eric Anthony.

4. On December 7, 2006, the Seattle Mariners traded Rafael Soriano to the Atlanta Braves for Horacio Ramirez.

5. On December 20, 1993, the Seattle Mariners traded Omar Vizquel to the Cleveland Indians for Reggie Jefferson, Felix Fermin, and cash considerations.

6. On December 7, 1995, the Seattle Mariners traded Tino Martinez, Jim Mercir, and Jeff Nelson to the New York Yankees for Russ Davis and Sterling Hitchcock.

7. On September 13, 1996, the Seattle Mariners traded David Ortiz (Yes, Big Papi!) to the Minnesota Twins to complete a deal made in August.

8. On July 31, 1997, the Seattle Mariners traded Jason Varitek and Derek Lowe to the Boston Red Sox for Heathcliff Slocumb.

9. The Seattle Mariners have made 17 trades with the Chicago Cubs.

10. The Seattle Mariners have made 16 trades with the Kansas City Royals.

CHAPTER 8:

DRAFT DAY

QUIZ TIME!

1. Ken Griffey Jr. was drafted in which position by the Seattle Mariners in the 1st round of the 1987 MLB Draft?

    a. 1st

    b. 2nd

    c. 3rd

    d. 4th

2. Randy Johnson was drafted by which team in the 2nd round of the 1985 MLB Draft?

    a. Seattle Mariners

    b. Arizona Diamondbacks

    c. Atlanta Braves

    d. Montreal Expos

3. With which overall pick in the 1st round of the 1993 MLB Draft did the Seattle Mariners select Alex Rodriguez?

    a. 1st

    b. 2nd

c. 3rd

d. 4th

4. Jamie Moyer was drafted in the 6th round of the 1984 MLB Draft by which team?

   a. Texas Rangers

   b. Philadelphia Phillies

   c. Chicago Cubs

   d. Seattle Mariners

5. The Seattle Mariners drafted Kyle Seager in which round of the 2009 MLB Draft?

   a. 2nd

   b. 3rd

   c. 4th

   d. 5th

6. Jay Buhner was drafted by which team in the 2nd round of the 1984 MLB Draft?

   a. New York Yankees

   b. Atlanta Braves

   c. Seattle Mariners

   d. Pittsburgh Pirates

7. Alvin Davis was drafted by the Seattle Mariners in the 6th round of the 1982 MLB Draft.

   a. True

   b. False

8. Bret Boone was drafted by the Seattle Mariners in which round of the 1990 MLB Draft?

a. 3rd

b. 4th

c. 5th

d. 6th

9. Mark Langston was drafted by the Seattle Mariners in which round of the 1981 MLB Draft?

    a. 1st

    b. 2nd

    c. 3rd

    d. 4th

10. Mike Cameron was drafted by the Chicago White Sox in the 18th round of the 1991 MLB Draft.

    a. True

    b. False

11. John Olerud was drafted by which team in the 3rd round of the 1989 MLB Draft?

    a. New York Yankees

    b. New York Mets

    c. Toronto Blue Jays

    d. Boston Red Sox

12. Erik Hanson was drafted by the Seattle Mariners in the 2nd round of the 1986 MLB Draft.

    a. True

    b. False

13. With which overall pick in the 1st round of the 1981 MLB Draft did the Seattle Mariners select Mike Moore?

a. 1st

b. 3rd

c. 5th

d. 8th

14. With which overall pick in the 1st round of the 1980 MLB Draft did the Seattle Mariners select Harold Reynolds?

a. 1st

b. 2nd

c. 5th

d. 6th

15. Raúl Ibañez was drafted by the Seattle Mariners in which round of the 1992 MLB Draft?

a. 6th

b. 16th

c. 26th

d. 36th

16. Rickey Henderson was drafted by the Oakland A's in which round of the 1976 MLB Draft?

a. 1st

b. 2nd

c. 3rd

d. 4th

17. Michael Saunders was drafted in the 11th round of which MLB Draft by the Seattle Mariners?

a. 1999

b. 2001

c. 2004

d. 2005

18. Justin Smoak was drafted in the 1st round, with which overall pick, of the 2008 MLB Draft by the Texas Rangers?

    a. 10th

    b. 11th

    c. 12th

    d. 13th

19. Chone Figgins was drafted in the 4th round of the 1997 MLB Draft by which team?

    a. San Diego Padres

    b. Los Angeles Dodgers

    c. Los Angeles Angels of Anaheim

    d. Colorado Rockies

20. Tino Martinez was drafted by the Seattle Mariners in the 1st round, 14th overall, of the 1988 MLB Draft.

    a. True

    b. False

QUIZ ANSWERS

1. A – 1st

2. D – Montreal Expos

3. A – 1st

4. C – Chicago Cubs

5. B – 3rd

6. D – Pittsburgh Pirates

7. A – True

8. C – 5th

9. B – 2nd

10. A – True

11. C – Toronto Blue Jays

12. A – True

13. A – 1st

14. B – 2nd

15. D – 36th

16. D – 4th

17. C – 2004

18. B – 11th

19. D – Colorado Rockies

20. A – True

DID YOU KNOW?

1. Dave Henderson was drafted in the 1st round (26th overall) of the 1977 MLB Draft by the Seattle Mariners.

2. Goose Gossage was drafted in the 9th round of the 1970 MLB Draft by the Chicago White Sox.

3. Rick Honeycutt was drafted in the 17th round of the 1976 MLB Draft by the Pittsburgh Pirates.

4. Willie Bloomquist was drafted in the 3rd round of the 1999 MLB Draft by the Seattle Mariners.

5. J.J. Putz was drafted in the 6th round of the 1999 MLB Draft by the Seattle Mariners.

6. Jason Vargas was drafted in the 2nd round of the 2004 MLB Draft by the Florida Marlins.

7. Taijuan Walker was drafted in the 1st round (43rd overall) of the 2010 MLB Draft by the Seattle Mariners.

8. Mike Zunino was drafted in the 1st round (3rd overall) of the 2012 MLB Draft by the Seattle Mariners.

9. Tom Wilhelmsen was drafted in the 7th round of the 2002 MLB Draft by the Milwaukee Brewers.

10. Dan Wilson was drafted in the 1st round (7th overall) of the 1990 MLB Draft by the Cincinnati Reds.

CHAPTER 9:

ODDS & ENDS

QUIZ TIME!

1. Which former Mariner coached the American League in the 2010 Taco Bell All-Star Legends & Celebrity Softball Game?

    a. Ken Griffey Jr.
    b. Edgar Martinez
    c. Goose Gossage
    d. Alex Rodriguez

2. Former Mariner Robinson Cano was named after Jackie Robinson.

    a. True
    b. False

3. Jamie Moyer and his ex-wife Karen were introduced by which famous baseball broadcaster?

    a. Vin Scully
    b. Bob Uecker
    c. Harry Caray
    d. Tim McCarver

4. Adrian Beltre hates when people touch which part of him?

   a. Feet
   b. Shoulder
   c. Ear
   d. Head

5. What is the name of the 2011 baseball documentary starring R.A. Dickey?

   a. *Four Days in October*
   b. *Screwball*
   c. *Knuckleball*
   d. *No-No*

6. Mark Langston appeared in a 1997 episode of which popular television show, entitled "To Tell a Mortal"?

   a. *The Fresh Prince of Bel Air*
   b. *Home Improvement*
   c. *Full House*
   d. *Sabrina, the Teenage Witch*

7. John Olerud is the cousin of fellow MLB player Dale Sveum.

   a. True
   b. False

8. Which former MLB player was Kyle Seager's idol while growing up?

   a. Frank Thomas
   b. Chipper Jones

c. Derek Jeter

d. Ken Griffey Jr.

9. Lou Piniella made a cameo in which baseball film?

  a. *Moneyball*

  b. *Little Big League*

  c. *Fever Pitch*

  d. *The Rookie*

10. Which former Mariner was named the second nicest player in the MLB in a poll by *Sports Illustrated*?

  a. Ken Griffey Jr.

  b. Raúl Ibañez

  c. Alvin Davis

  d. Jay Buhner

11. Danny Tartabull made appearances as himself in two episodes of which sitcom?

  a. *Everybody Loves Raymond*

  b. *The King of Queens*

  c. *Fresh Prince of Bel Air*

  d. *Seinfeld*

12. Rickey Henderson is known for referring to himself in the third person.

  a. True

  b. False

13. Rick Honeycutt was the pitching coach for which team from 2006 to 2019?

a. St. Louis Cardinals

b. Oakland A's

c. Los Angeles Dodgers

d. Texas Rangers

14. A song called "Wicked Gil" by Seattle rock group Band of Horses was inspired by Gil Meche.

a. True

b. False

15. Tom Paciorek is known by the nickname "Wimpy," which was given to him by which player at a dinner where he was the only one to order a burger when every other teammate ordered steak?

a. Sandy Koufax

b. Vin Scully

c. Tommy Lasorda

d. Kirk Gibson

16. J.J. Putz shared a dorm with NFL quarterback Tom Brady while at the University of Michigan.

a. True

b. False

17. While playing basketball at Santa Clara University, Randy Winn was teammates with which NBA star?

a. LeBron James

b. Steve Nash

c. Kobe Bryant

d. Steve Kerr

18. Ken Griffey Sr.'s father Buddy was high school teammates with which MLB legend?

    a. Mickey Mantle
    b. Ted Williams
    c. Jackie Robinson
    d. Stan Musial

19. In 2019, Eric Byrnes set the Guinness World Record for which feat?

    a. Fastest 100 meter hurdles wearing swim fins
    b. Most holes of golf in a single day
    c. Most pull-ups in 24 hours
    d. Fastest 50 meters walking on hands with a soccer ball between the legs

20. Ichiro Suzuki speaks English well, but he uses an interpreter during interviews so that he is not misunderstood.

    a. True
    b. False

QUIZ ANSWERS

1. C – Goose Gossage

2. A – True

3. C – Harry Caray

4. D – Head

5. C – *Knuckleball*

6. D – *Sabrina, the Teenage Witch*

7. A – True

8. C – Derek Jeter

9. B – *Little Big League*

10. B – Raúl Ibañez

11. D – *Seinfeld*

12. A – True

13. C – Los Angeles Dodgers

14. A – True

15. C – Tommy Lasorda

16. A – True

17. B – Steve Nash

18. D – Stan Musial

19. B – Most holes of golf in a single day (He played 420 holes, walking, in 24 hours.)

20. A – True

DID YOU KNOW?

1. Back in 1998, former Mariner Alex Rodriguez was asked by a reporter who his dream date would be with. His answer? Jennifer Lopez. And 23 years later, J-Lo and A-Rod were engaged to be married.

2. Former Mariner Nelson Cruz takes a nap before almost every game he plays in as a pregame ritual.

3. Former Mariner Harold Reynolds is currently a studio analyst, host, and sportscaster for MLB Network.

4. Adrian Beltre was once in a JCPenney Christmas commercial, but it was not planned. In fact, the people from JCPenney didn't recognize him or even realize it was him until the ad was released.

5. On the last day of the 1998 season, Bret Boone was a part of the only infield ever composed of two sets of brothers: first baseman Stephen Larkin, second baseman Bret Boone, shortstop Barry Larkin, and third baseman Aaron Boone.

6. Mike Cameron is the only MLB player to hit two home runs in the same game with eight different MLB teams.

7. Former Mariners manager Bob Melvin is the current manager of the AL West rival Oakland A's.

8. On August 12, 2015, Hisashi Iwakuma became the second Japanese player ever to pitch a no-hitter in the MLB

(joining Hideo Nomo, who threw two). He helped defeat the Baltimore Orioles at Safeco Field in that game.

9. On May 7, 2012, Omar Vizquel became the oldest player to play at shortstop in Major League Baseball history.

10. From 1997 to 2006, Dave Henderson worked as a color commentator during Mariners radio and television broadcasts.

CHAPTER 10:

OUTFIELDERS

QUIZ TIME!

1. Over the course of his 22-season MLB career, Ken Griffey Jr. played for the Seattle Mariners, Chicago White Sox, and which other team?

    a. San Diego Padres

    b. Cincinnati Reds

    c. Oakland A's

    d. Colorado Rockies

2. Ichiro Suzuki was named to 10 MLB All-Star Games during his 19-season MLB career.

    a. True

    b. False

3. How many seasons did Jay Buhner spend with the Seattle Mariners?

    a. 12

    b. 13

    c. 14

    d. 15

4. Mike Cameron won three Gold Glove Awards during his 17-season MLB career.

   a. True
   b. False

5. How many Silver Slugger Awards has Nelson Cruz won so far in his career?

   a. 1
   b. 2
   c. 3
   d. 4

6. Which of the following teams did former Mariner Raúl Ibañez NOT play for during his 19-season MLB career?

   a. New York Yankees
   b. Kansas City Royals
   c. Milwaukee Brewers
   d. Philadelphia Phillies

7. Franklin Gutierrez played seven seasons with the Seattle Mariners.

   a. True
   b. False

8. How many MLB All-Star Games was Dave Henderson named to during his 14-season MLB career?

   a. 0
   b. 1
   c. 2
   d. 3

9. What year was Rickey Henderson inducted into the National Baseball Hall of Fame?

   a. 2008
   b. 2009
   c. 2010
   d. 2011

10. How many MLB All-Star Games was Michael Saunders named to during his nine-year MLB career?

   a. 0
   b. 1
   c. 2
   d. 3

11. Vince Coleman was named National League Rookie of the Year for which year?

   a. 1983
   b. 1984
   c. 1985
   d. 1986

12. Ruppert Jones was named to two MLB All-Star Games during his 12-season MLB career.

   a. True
   b. False

13. How many seasons did Rich Amaral spend with the Seattle Mariners?

   a. 5
   b. 6

c. 7

d. 8

14. How many MLB All-Star Games has Mitch Haniger been named to so far in his MLB career?

   a. 1

   b. 2

   c. 3

   d. 4

15. Which of the following teams did former Mariner Denard Span NOT play for during his 11-season MLB career?

   a. Washington Nationals

   b. Atlanta Braves

   c. Minnesota Twins

   d. Tampa Bay Rays

16. How many seasons did Henry Cotto spend with the Seattle Mariners?

   a. 3

   b. 4

   c. 5

   d. 6

17. Jeff Burroughs was named the American League MVP for which year?

   a. 1972

   b. 1973

   c. 1974

   d. 1975

18. How many MLB All-Star Games was Tom Paciorek named to during his 18-season MLB career?

    a. 0
    b. 1
    c. 3
    d. 5

19. Which of the following teams did former Mariner Leonys Martín NOT play for during his nine-season MLB career?

    a. Texas Rangers
    b. Cleveland Indians
    c. Houston Astros
    d. Chicago Cubs

20. Kevin Mitchell was named the 1989 National League MVP.

    a. True
    b. False

QUIZ ANSWERS

1. B – Cincinnati Reds

2. A – True

3. C – 14

4. A – True

5. D – 4

6. C – Milwaukee Brewers

7. A – True

8. B – 1

9. B – 2009

10. B – 1

11. C – 1985

12. A – True

13. D – 8

14. A – 1

15. B – Atlanta Braves

16. D – 6

17. C – 1974

18. B – 1

19. C – Houston Astros

20. A – True

DID YOU KNOW?

1. Ken Griffey Jr. spent 13 seasons of his MLB career with the Seattle Mariners. He also played for the Cincinnati Reds and Chicago White Sox. He is a member of the National Baseball Hall of Fame, MVP, thirteen-time MLB All-Star, ten-time Gold Glove Award winner, seven-time Silver Slugger Award winner, All-Star MVP, and Major League Player of the Year.

2. Ichiro Suzuki spent 14 seasons of his MLB career with the Seattle Mariners. He also played for the New York Yankees and Miami Marlins. He is an MVP, American League Rookie of the Year, ten-time MLB All-Star, ten-time Gold Glove Award winner, three-time Silver Slugger Award winner, two-time batting title champion, and All-Star MVP.

3. Jay Buhner spent 14 seasons of his 15-season MLB career with the Seattle Mariners. He also played for the New York Yankees. He is a one-time MLB All-Star and one-time Gold Glove Award winner.

4. Mike Cameron spent four seasons of his 17-season MLB career with the Seattle Mariners. He also played for the Chicago White Sox, New York Mets, Boston Red Sox, San Diego Padres, Milwaukee Brewers, Cincinnati Reds, and Florida Marlins. He is a three-time Gold Glove Award winner and one-time MLB All-Star.

5. Rickey Henderson only spent one season with the Seattle Mariners out of his 25 seasons spent in the MLB. He also played for the Oakland Athletics, New York Yankees, San Diego Padres, New York Mets, Boston Red Sox, Los Angeles Dodgers, Anaheim Angels, and Toronto Blue Jays. He is a member of the National Baseball Hall of Fame, 1990 American League MVP, 1989 ALCS MVP, ten-time MLB All-Star, two-time World Series champion, one-time Gold Glove Award winner, three-time Silver Slugger Award winner, and holds all-time career records in stolen bases and runs scored.

6. Kevin Mitchell spent one season of his 13-season MLB career with the Seattle Mariners. He also played for the San Francisco Giants, Cincinnati Reds, New York Mets, Oakland A's, Boston Red Sox, San Diego Padres, and Cleveland Indians. He is an MVP, two-time MLB All-Star, 1986 World Series champion, one-time Silver Slugger Award winner, and Major League Player of the Year.

7. Franklin Gutierrez spent seven seasons of his 12-season MLB career with the Seattle Mariners. He also played for the Cleveland Indians and Los Angeles Dodgers. He is a one-time Gold Glove Award winner.

8. Tom Paciorek spent four seasons of his 18-season MLB career with the Seattle Mariners. He also played for the Los Angeles Dodgers, Chicago White Sox, Atlanta Braves, Texas Rangers, and New York Mets. He is a one-time MLB All-Star.

9. Jeff Burroughs spent one season of his 16-season MLB career with the Seattle Mariners. He also played for the Atlanta Braves, Oakland A's, Texas Rangers, and Toronto Blue Jays. He is an MVP and two-time MLB All-Star.

10. Nelson Cruz spent four seasons of his MLB career with the Seattle Mariners and currently plays for the Minnesota Twins. So far in his career, he has also played for the Texas Rangers, Minnesota Twins, and Baltimore Orioles. As of the end of the 2020 season, he is a six-time MLB All-Star, four-time Silver Slugger Award winner, and ALCS MVP.

CHAPTER 11:

INFIELDERS

QUIZ TIME!

1. How many MLB All-Star Games was Alex Rodriguez named to during his 22-season MLB career?

   a. 12
   b. 13
   c. 14
   d. 15

2. Edgar Martinez was inducted into the National Baseball Hall of Fame in 2019.

   a. True
   b. False

3. As of the end of the 2020 season, how many Gold Glove Awards has Kyle Seager won in his MLB career?

   a. 0
   b. 1
   c. 2
   d. 3

4. As of the end of the 2020 season, how many Silver Slugger Awards has Robinson Cano won in his MLB career?

    a. 1
    b. 2
    c. 3
    d. 5

5. Kyle Seager's brother, Corey Seager, currently plays for which MLB team?

    a. Washington Nationals
    b. Toronto Blue Jays
    c. Oakland A's
    d. Los Angeles Dodgers

6. How many Platinum Glove Awards did Adrian Beltre win during his 21-season MLB career?

    a. 1
    b. 2
    c. 3
    d. 4

7. Alvin Davis was named the 1984 American League Rookie of the Year.

    a. True
    b. False

8. How many Gold Glove Awards did Bret Boone win during his 14-season MLB career?

    a. 2
    b. 3

c. 4

d. 5

9. How many MLB All-Star Games was John Olerud named to during his 17-season MLB career?

    a. 1

    b. 2

    c. 3

    d. 4

10. How many Gold Glove Awards did Harold Reynolds win during his 12-season MLB career?

    a. 0

    b. 1

    c. 2

    d. 3

11. How many All-Star Games was Tino Martinez named to during his 16-season MLB career?

    a. 1

    b. 2

    c. 3

    d. 4

12. Justin Smoak spent five seasons with the Seattle Mariners.

    a. True

    b. False

13. Which of the following teams did former Mariner Joey Cora NOT play for during his 11-season MLB career?

a. Chicago White Sox

b. San Diego Padres

c. Cleveland Indians

d. Tampa Bay Devil Rays

14. How many All-Star Games was Chone Figgins named to during his 12-season MLB career?

a. 0

b. 1

c. 2

d. 3

15. Over the course of his 14-season MLB career, Carlos Guillen spent six years with the Seattle Mariners and eight seasons with which team?

a. Florida Marlins

b. New York Yankees

c. Detroit Tigers

d. Chicago White Sox

16. Alex Rodriguez won 10 Silver Slugger Awards during his MLB career.

a. True

b. False

17. How many Gold Glove Awards did Omar Vizquel win during his 24-season MLB career?

a. 8

b. 9

c. 10

d. 11

18. How many Silver Slugger Awards did Adrian Beltre win during his 21-season MLB career?

    a. 1
    b. 2
    c. 3
    d. 4

19. Alvin Davis spent eight seasons with the Seattle Mariners and one season with which team?

    a. St. Louis Cardinals
    b. Houston Astros
    c. California Angels
    d. Oakland A's

20. Harold Reynolds played his entire 12-season MLB career with the Seattle Mariners.

    a. True
    b. False

QUIZ ANSWERS

1. C – 14

2. A – True

3. B – 1

4. D – 5

5. D – Los Angeles Dodgers

6. B – 2

7. A – True

8. C – 4

9. B – 2

10. D – 3

11. B – 2

12. A – True

13. D – Tampa Bay Devil Rays

14. B – 1

15. C – Detroit Tigers

16. A – True

17. D – 11

18. D – 4

19. C – California Angels

20. B – False (He played for the Mariners, Baltimore Orioles, and California Angels.)

DID YOU KNOW?

1. Edgar Martinez spent his entire 18-season MLB career with the Seattle Mariners. He is a member of the National Baseball Hall of Fame, seven-time MLB All-Star, five-time Silver Slugger Award winner, and two-time batting title champion.

2. Alex Rodriguez spent seven seasons of his 22-season MLB career with the Seattle Mariners. He also played for the New York Yankees and Texas Rangers. He is a three-time MVP, fourteen-time MLB All-Star, World Series champion, two-time Gold Glove Award winner, ten-time Silver Slugger Award winner, batting title champion, and two-time Major League Player of the Year.

3. Adrian Beltre spent five seasons of his 21-season MLB career with the Seattle Mariners. He also played for the Texas Rangers, Los Angeles Dodgers, and Boston Red Sox. He is a four-time MLB All-Star, five-time Gold Glove Award winner, four-time Silver Slugger Award winner, and two-time Platinum Glove Award winner.

4. Harold Reynolds spent 10 seasons of his 12-season MLB career with the Seattle Mariners. He also played for the California Angels and Baltimore Orioles. He is a two-time MLB All-Star and three-time Gold Glove Award winner.

5. John Olerud spent five seasons of his 17-season MLB career with the Seattle Mariners. He also played for the

Toronto Blue Jays, New York Mets, New York Yankees, and Boston Red Sox. He is a two-time MLB All-Star, two-time World Series champion, three-time Gold Glove Award winner, and batting title champion.

6. Robinson Cano spent five seasons of his MLB career with the Seattle Mariners. He has also played for the New York Yankees. He currently plays for the New York Mets. So far in his career, he is an eight-time MLB All-Star, World Series champion, two-time Gold Glove Award winner, five-time Silver Slugger Award winner, and All-Star MVP.

7. Kyle Seager has currently spent his entire MLB career with the Seattle Mariners and is a one-time MLB All-Star and one-time Gold Glove Award winner.

8. Omar Vizquel spent five seasons of his 24-season MLB career with the Seattle Mariners. He also played for the Cleveland Indians, San Francisco Giants, Chicago White Sox, Texas Rangers, and Toronto Blue Jays. He is a three-time MLB All-Star and eleven-time Gold Glove Award winner.

9. Alvin Davis spent eight seasons of his nine-season MLB career with the Seattle Mariners. He also played for the California Angels. He is a one-time MLB All-Star and American League Rookie of the Year.

10. Tino Martinez spent six seasons of his 16-season MLB career with the Seattle Mariners. He also played for the New York Yankees, St. Louis Cardinals, and Tampa Bay

Devil Rays. He is a two-time MLB All-Star, one-time Silver Slugger Award winner, and four-time World Series champion.

CHAPTER 12:

PITCHERS & CATCHERS

QUIZ TIME!

1. What year was Randy Johnson inducted into the National Baseball Hall of Fame?

    a. 2012

    b. 2014

    c. 2015

    d. 2018

2. Felix Hernandez spent 15 seasons of his MLB career with the Seattle Mariners.

    a. True

    b. False

3. How many seasons of his MLB career did Jamie Moyer spend with the Seattle Mariners?

    a. 8

    b. 9

    c. 10

    d. 11

4. How many Gold Glove Awards did Mark Langston win during his 16-season MLB career?

    a. 5
    b. 6
    c. 7
    d. 8

5. Freddy Garcia won the American League ERA Title in which year?

    a. 2000
    b. 2001
    c. 2002
    d. 2003

6. Mike Moore spent seven seasons of his MLB career with the Seattle Mariners, three seasons with the Detroit Tigers, and four seasons with which other team?

    a. Los Angeles Dodgers
    b. Oakland A's
    c. Minnesota Twins
    d. Texas Rangers

7. Dan Wilson spent 12 seasons with the Seattle Mariners.

    a. True
    b. False

8. How many MLB All-Star Games was Rick Honeycutt named to during his 21-season MLB career?

    a. 1
    b. 2

c. 3

d. 4

9. How many All-Star Games was Cliff Lee named to during his 13-season MLB career?

    a. 1

    b. 2

    c. 3

    d. 4

10. How many All-Star Games was Terry Mulholland named to during his 20-season MLB career?

    a. 1

    b. 2

    c. 5

    d. 6

11. How many MLB All-Star Games was J.J. Putz named to over the course of his 12-season MLB career?

    a. 0

    b. 1

    c. 2

    d. 3

12. Eddie Guardado was named to two All-Star Games during his 17-season MLB career.

    a. True

    b. False

13. Which of the following teams did former Mariner Aaron Sele NOT play for during his 15-season MLB career?

a. Boston Red Sox

b. Anaheim Angels

c. Texas Rangers

d. Florida Marlins

14. Which of the following teams did former Mariner Mike Morgan NOT play for during his 22-season MLB career?

    a. Chicago Cubs

    b. Boston Red Sox

    c. Oakland A's

    d. Arizona Diamondbacks

15. Glenn Abbott spent six seasons with the Seattle Mariners, four seasons with the Oakland A's, and two seasons with which other team?

    a. Cincinnati Reds

    b. Baltimore Orioles

    c. Detroit Tigers

    d. Montreal Expos

16. Former Mariners pitcher Bud Black is the current manager of the Colorado Rockies.

    a. True

    b. False

17. What year was Gaylord Perry inducted into the National Baseball Hall of Fame?

    a. 1990

    b. 1991

    c. 1992

    d. 1993

18. Which of the following teams did former Mariner Floyd Bannister NOT play for during his 15-season MLB career?

    a. Chicago White Sox
    b. Kansas City Royals
    c. Houston Astros
    d. Chicago Cubs

19. What year was Rich "Goose" Gossage inducted into the National Baseball Hall of Fame?

    a. 2006
    b. 2007
    c. 2008
    d. 2009

20. Mike Zunino spent six seasons with the Seattle Mariners.

    a. True
    b. False

QUIZ ANSWERS

1. C – 2015

2. A – True

3. D – 11

4. C – 7

5. B – 2001

6. B – Oakland A's

7. A – True

8. B – 2

9. D – 4

10. A – 1

11. B – 1

12. A – True

13. D – Florida Marlins

14. B – Boston Red Sox

15. C – Detroit Tigers

16. A – True

17. B – 1991

18. D – Chicago Cubs

19. C – 2008

20. A – True

DID YOU KNOW?

1. Randy Johnson spent 10 seasons of his 22-season MLB career with the Seattle Mariners. He also played for the Arizona Diamondbacks, Montreal Expos, New York Yankees, San Francisco Giants, and Houston Astros. He is a member of the National Baseball Hall of Fame, five-time Cy Young Award winner, Triple Crown winner, ten-time MLB All-Star, World Series champion, World Series MVP, and four-time ERA Title winner.

2. Felix Hernandez spent 15 seasons of his MLB career with the Seattle Mariners. He currently plays for the Baltimore Orioles. He is a Cy Young Award winner, six-time MLB All-Star, and two-time ERA Title winner.

3. Jamie Moyer spent 11 seasons of his 25-season MLB career with the Seattle Mariners. He also played for the Philadelphia Phillies, Colorado Rockies, Chicago Cubs, Baltimore Orioles, Texas Rangers, St. Louis Cardinals, and Boston Red Sox. He is a one-time MLB All-Star and World Series champion.

4. Mark Langston spent six seasons of his 16-season MLB career with the Seattle Mariners. He also played for the Anaheim Angels, San Diego Padres, Cleveland Indians, and Montreal Expos. He is a four-time MLB All-Star and seven-time Gold Glove Award winner.

5. Rick Honeycutt spent four seasons of his 21-season MLB career with the Seattle Mariners. He also played for the Oakland A's, Los Angeles Dodgers, Texas Rangers, St. Louis Cardinals, and New York Yankees. He is a two-time MLB All-Star, one-time World Series champion, and one-time ERA Title winner.

6. Gaylord Perry spent two seasons of his 22-season MLB career with the Seattle Mariners. He also played for the San Francisco Giants, Texas Rangers, Cleveland Indians, San Diego Padres, Kansas City Royals, Atlanta Braves, and New York Yankees. He is a member of the National Baseball Hall of Fame, two-time Cy Young Award winner, and five-time MLB All-Star.

7. Rich "Goose" Gossage spent one season of his 22-season MLB career with the Seattle Mariners. He also played for the New York Yankees, Oakland A's, Chicago White Sox, San Diego Padres, San Francisco Giants, Pittsburgh Pirates, Texas Rangers, and Chicago Cubs. He is a member of the National Baseball Hall of Fame, nine-time MLB All-Star, World Series champion, and the 1978 Rolaids Relief Man winner (reliever of the year).

8. Dan Wilson spent 12 seasons of his 14-season MLB career with the Seattle Mariners. He also played for the Cincinnati Reds. He is a one-time All-Star.

9. Freddy Garcia spent six seasons of his 15-season MLB career with the Seattle Mariners. He also played for the Chicago White Sox, New York Yankees, Atlanta Braves,

Philadelphia Phillies, Baltimore Orioles, and Detroit Tigers. He is a two-time MLB All-Star, one-time World Series champion, and one-time ERA Title winner.

10. J.J. Putz spent six seasons of his 12-season MLB career with the Seattle Mariners. He also played for the Arizona Diamondbacks, New York Mets, and Chicago White Sox. He is a one-time MLB All-Star and Rolaids Relief Man winner (reliever of the year).

CHAPTER 13:

ICHIRO

QUIZ TIME!

1. Where was Ichiro Suzuki born?

    a. Osaka, Japan
    b. Tokyo, Japa
    c. Nagoya, Japan
    d. Higashi Yamoto, Japan

2. Ichiro Suzuki was the first MLB player to enter the Japanese Baseball Hall of Fame.

    a. True
    b. False

3. How many Silver Slugger Awards did Ichiro Suzuki win during his 19-season MLB career?

    a. 0
    b. 1
    c. 2
    d. 3

4. How many Gold Glove Awards did Ichiro Suzuki win during his MLB career?

    a. 3
    b. 6
    c. 10
    d. 14

5. How many MLB All-Star Games was Ichiro Suzuki named to during his MLB career?

    a. 5
    b. 8
    c. 10
    d. 12

6. Ichiro Suzuki was named the American League Rookie of the Year in which year?

    a. 2000
    b. 2001
    c. 2002
    d. 2003

7. Ichiro Suzuki spent his entire MLB career with the Seattle Mariners.

    a. True
    b. False

8. What is Ichiro Suzuki's career batting average?

    a. .281
    b. .291
    c. .301
    d. .311

9. How many home runs did Ichiro Suzuki hit during his MLB career?

   a. 117
   b. 127
   c. 137
   d. 147

10. How many RBIs did Ichiro Suzuki collect during his MLB career?

   a. 480
   b. 580
   c. 680
   d. 780

11. How many hits did Ichiro Suzuki collect during his MLB career?

   a. 2,989
   b. 3,089
   c. 3,189
   d. 3,289

12. Ichiro Suzuki did NOT win a World Series championship during his MLB career.

   a. True
   b. False

13. Ichiro Suzuki was the American League batting champion in 2001 and again in which year?

   a. 2002
   b. 2003

c. 2004

d. 2005

14. Ichiro Suzuki was the American League stolen base leader in which year?

    a. 2001

    b. 2002

    c. 2003

    d. 2004

15. Ichiro Suzuki was named the AL MVP in which year?

    a. 2001

    b. 2005

    c. 2007

    d. 2008

16. Ichiro Suzuki stole 509 bases during his MLB career.

    a. True

    b. False

17. How many seasons did Ichiro Suzuki spend with the Seattle Mariners?

    a. 10

    b. 12

    c. 14

    d. 16

18. How many seasons did Ichiro Suzuki spend with the New York Yankees?

    a. 2

    b. 3

c. 4

d. 5

19. How many seasons did Ichiro Suzuki spend with the Miami Marlins?

    a. 1

    b. 2

    c. 3

    d. 4

20. Ichiro Suzuki holds the MLB record for hits in a single season with 262 in 2004.

    a. True

    b. False

QUIZ ANSWERS

1. C – Nagoya, Japan

2. A – True

3. D – 3 (2001, 2007, 2009)

4. C – 10 (2001 to 2010 consecutively)

5. C – 10 (2001 to 2010 consecutively)

6. B – 2001

7. B – False (He played for the Mariners, Yankees, and Marlins.)

8. D – .311

9. A – 117

10. D – 780

11. B – 3,089

12. A – True

13. C – 2004

14. A – 2001

15. A – 2001

16. A – True

17. C – 14

18. B – 3

19. C – 3

20. A – True

DID YOU KNOW?

1. Before coming to the MLB, Ichiro Suzuki spent nine seasons with the Orix BlueWave of Nippon Professional Baseball (NPB) in Japan.

2. Ichiro Suzuki has recorded the most hits of all Japanese-born players in MLB history.

3. Ichiro Suzuki was named the April, May, August, and September AL Rookie of the Month during the 2001 season. He was named the AL Player of the Month in August of 2004.

4. Ichiro Suzuki was named the AL Player of the Week five times during his MLB career.

5. Ichiro Suzuki was named the 2007 All-Star Game MVP.

6. Ichiro Suzuki used his first name on the back of his uniform instead of his last name, becoming the first player in Major League Baseball to do so since Vida Blue.

7. According to *Forbes*, at the height of his career, Ichiro Suzuki earned roughly $7 million a year from endorsements, most of which came from Japanese companies.

8. On June 25, 2017, Ichiro (at age 43 years and 246 days) became the oldest player to start a game in center field since at least 1900, breaking the record previously held by Rickey Henderson.

9. On April 19, 2017, Ichiro hit his first home run against the Seattle Mariners.

10. Due to a previous agreement between Japanese baseball and the MLB, Ichiro was not allowed to play in the United States until 2001.

CHAPTER 14:

HEATED RIVALRIES

QUIZ TIME!

1. Which team does NOT play in the American League West with the Seattle Mariners?

   a. Oakland A's
   b. Houston Astros
   c. Kansas City Royals
   d. Los Angeles Angels

2. The Kansas City Royals, Chicago White Sox, and Minnesota Twins all moved from the AL West to the AL Central in 1994.

   a. True
   b. False

3. Which team below was once a member of the AL West Division?

   a. Cleveland Indians
   b. Los Angeles Dodgers
   c. Detroit Tigers
   d. Milwaukee Brewers

4. What current American League West team has the most AL West championships?

   a. Seattle Mariners
   b. Oakland A's
   c. Texas Rangers
   d. Los Angeles Angels

5. Which current AL West team moved to the division in 2013?

   a. Texas Rangers
   b. Los Angeles Angels
   c. Houston Astros
   d. Oakland A's

6. Which AL West team won the division most recently in 2020?

   a. Seattle Mariners
   b. Los Angeles Angels
   c. Houston Astros
   d. Oakland A's

7. The Seattle Mariners' most recent AL West championship was in 2001.

   a. True
   b. False

8. The Seattle Mariners have not won a World Series championship in franchise history so far. How many have the Oakland A's won?

   a. 3
   b. 5

c. 6

d. 9

9. The Seattle Mariners have not won a World Series championship in franchise history so far. How many have the Los Angeles Angels won?

    a. 0

    b. 1

    c. 2

    d. 3

10. The Seattle Mariners have not won a World Series championship in franchise history so far. How many have the Texas Rangers won?

    a. 0

    b. 1

    c. 2

    d. 3

11. The Seattle Mariners have not won a World Series championship in franchise history so far. How many have the Houston Astros won?

    a. 0

    b. 1

    c. 2

    d. 3

12. The Houston Astros and Seattle Mariners are tied for the least AL West championships with three each (as of the end of the 2020 season).

a. True

b. False

13. Which player has NOT played for both the Mariners and the Oakland A's?

    a. Rick Honeycutt

    b. Rickey Henderson

    c. Ken Griffey Jr.

    d. Dave Henderson

14. Which player has NOT played for both the Mariners and the Los Angeles Angels?

    a. Chone Figgins

    b. Mike Moore

    c. Raúl Ibañez

    d. Mark Trumbo

15. Which player has NOT played for both the Mariners and the Texas Rangers?

    a. Adrian Beltre

    b. Goose Gossage

    c. Mike Cameron

    d. Omar Vizquel

16. Before the Houston Astros moved to the division in 2013, the AL West was the only MLB division with four teams.

    a. True

    b. False

17. Which player has NOT played for both the Mariners and the Houston Astros?

a. Doug Fister

b. Harold Reynolds

c. Randy Johnson

d. Rusty Meacham

18. The Seattle Mariners have won three AL West division championships so far in franchise history. How many have the Oakland A's won?

a. 15

b. 16

c. 17

d. 18

19. The Seattle Mariners have won three AL West division championships so far in franchise history. How many have the Los Angeles Angels won?

a. 6

b. 7

c. 8

d. 9

20. The Seattle Mariners have won three AL West division championships so far in franchise history. The Texas Rangers have won seven.

a. True

b. False

QUIZ ANSWERS

1. C – Kansas City Royals

2. A – True

3. D – Milwaukee Brewers

4. B – Oakland A's

5. C – Houston Astros

6. D – Oakland A's

7. A – True

8. D – 9

9. B – 1

10. A – 0

11. B – 1

12. A – True

13. C – Ken Griffey Jr.

14. B – Mike Moore

15. C – Mike Cameron

16. A – True

17. B – Harold Reynolds

18. C – 17

19. D – 9

20. A – True

DID YOU KNOW?

1. The Oakland A's have the most American League West championships, with 17 (as of the end of the 2020 season). The Los Angeles Angels have nine, the Texas Rangers have seven, and the Seattle Mariners and Houston Astros have three each. Former teams of the division who won AL West championships include: Kansas City Royals (6), Minnesota Twins (4), and Chicago White Sox (2). Another former AL West team, the Milwaukee Brewers never won a division championship. The most recent AL West Division champions are the Oakland A's (2020). The Mariners have not won the AL West since 2001 (as of the end of the 2020 season).

2. In 1995, the Seattle Mariners and California Angels were tied for the AL West division championship and played in a tie-breaker game. The Mariners won 9-1 and, therefore, won the division.

3. Currently, AL West teams reside on the West Coast and in Texas. In the past, the American League West Division has had teams as far east as Chicago.

4. The AL West was founded in 1969 and consisted of the Oakland A's, California Angels, Chicago White Sox, Kansas City Royals, Minnesota Twins, and Milwaukee Brewers (as the Seattle Pilots). Only the A's and Angels are still currently members of the AL West.

5. When the MLB split into two leagues in 1969, the six teams located in the Eastern Time Zone were placed in the East Division, while the other six were placed in the West Division.

6. Danny Espinosa, Chone Figgins, Brian Fuentes, Rickey Henderson, Chirs Ianetta, Raúl Ibañez, Adam Kennedy, Casey Kotchman, Mark Langston, Cameron Maybin, Kendrys Morales, Harold Reynolds, Mark Trumbo, Bobby Valentine, Jason Vargas, Fernando Rodney, and Jarrod Washburn have all played for both the Mariners and Los Angeles Angels.

7. Floyd Bannister, Adrian Beltre, Endy Chavez, Shin-Soo Choo, Larry Cox, Nelson Cruz, Doug Fister, Goose Gossage, Rick Honeycutt, Cliff Lee, Leonys Martín, Jamie Moyer, Gaylord Perry, Tom Paciorek, Alex Rodriguez, Justin Smoak, Omar Vizquel, and Tom Wilhelmsen have all played for both the Mariners and Texas Rangers.

8. Milton Bradley, Eric Byrnes, Ray Fosse, Goose Gossage, Dave Henderson, Rickey Henderson, Rick Honeycutt, Stan Javier, Kevin Mitchell, Mike Moore, Kendrys Morales, Fernando Rodney, Seth Smith, Dale Sveum, Danny Tartabull, Danny Valencia, and Casper Wells have all played for both the Mariners and the Oakland A's.

9. Floyd Bannister, Doug Fister, Stan Javier, Randy Johnson, Cameron Maybin, Wade Miley, and Mike Stanton have all played for the Mariners and the Houston Astros.

117

10. The Seattle Mariners joined the AL West in 1977 as an expansion team. They joined the Oakland A's, California Angels, Minnesota Twins, Chicago White Sox, Texas Rangers, and Kansas City Royals.

CHAPTER 15:

THE AWARDS SECTION

QUIZ TIME!

1. Which Seattle Mariners player won the American League MVP Award in 2001?

   a. John Olerud
   b. Ichiro Suzuki
   c. Edgar Martinez
   d. Jay Buhner

2. As of the end of the 2020 season, Lou Piniella is the only Seattle Mariners manager to ever win the American League Manager of the Year Award.

   a. True
   b. False

3. Which Seattle Mariners pitcher won an American League Cy Young Award in 2010?

   a. Doug Fister
   b. Cliff Lee
   c. Jason Vargas
   d. Felix Hernandez

4. Which Seattle Mariners player most recently won the American League Rookie of the Year Award (as of the end of the 2020 season)?

   a. Alvin Davis

   b. Ichiro Suzuki

   c. Kyle Lewis

   d. Kyle Seager

5. Which Seattle Mariners pitcher won the American League Reliever of the Year Award in 2018?

   a. James Pazos

   b. Edwin Diaz

   c. Chasen Bradford

   d. Alex Colome

6. Which Seattle Mariners player won a Silver Slugger Award in 2017?

   a. Mitch Haniger

   b. Kyle Seager

   c. Robinson Cano

   d. Nelson Cruz

7. No Seattle Mariners player has ever won the MLB Home Run Derby.

   a. True

   b. False

8. Which Seattle Mariners player was named the DHL Hometown Hero? (Voted by MLB fans as the most outstanding player in franchise history.)

a. Edgar Martinez
b. Ichiro Suzuki
c. Ken Griffey Jr.
d. Jay Buhner

9. Who was the first Seattle Mariners player to win an American League Gold Glove Award?

a. Mark Langston
b. Harold Reynolds
c. Omar Vizquel
d. Ken Griffey Jr.

10. Who was the first Seattle Mariners player to win a Silver Slugger Award?

a. Edgar Martinez
b. Ken Griffey Jr.
c. Alex Rodriguez
d. Bret Boone

11. Which Seattle Mariners player won the Wilson Defensive Player of the Year Award in 2012?

a. Chone Figgins
b. Kyle Seager
c. Dustin Ackley
d. Brendan Ryan

12. Ken Griffey Jr. won the 1998 ESPN ESPY Award for Best Male Athlete.

a. True
b. False

13. Alvin Davis was named the American League Rookie of the Year in which year?

   a. 1983
   b. 1984
   c. 1985
   d. 1986

14. Who was named the MLB All-Star Game MVP in 2017?

   a. Robinson Cano
   b. Kyle Seager
   c. Nelson Cruz
   d. Mike Zunino

15. How many Gold Glove Awards did Ichiro Suzuki win during his time with the Seattle Mariners?

   a. 6
   b. 8
   c. 10
   d. 12

16. Jamie Moyer won the 2003 Roberto Clemente Award.

   a. True
   b. False

17. Who was named the 2000 American League Rookie of the Year?

   a. Raúl Ibañez
   b. Alex Rodriguez
   c. Kazuhiro Sasaki
   d. Edgar Martinez

18. Which Seattle Mariners player won a Silver Slugger Award in 2000?

    a. Edgar Martinez
    b. Bret Boone
    c. Ichiro Suzuki
    d. Alex Rodriguez

19. Which Seattle Mariners player was given the 1995 American League Cy Young Award?

    a. Tim Belcher
    b. Randy Johnson
    c. Chris Bosio
    d. Andy Benes

20. J.J. Putz was named the 2007 American League Reliever of the Year.

    a. True
    b. False

QUIZ ANSWERS

1. B – Ichiro Suzuki

2. A – True (He won twice, in 1995 and 2001.)

3. D – Felix Hernandez

4. C – Kyle Lewis (2020)

5. B – Edwin Diaz

6. D – Nelson Cruz

7. B – False (Ken Griffey Jr. won the derby three times, in 1994, 1998, and 1999.)

8. C – Ken Griffey Jr.

9. A – Mark Langston (1987)

10. B – Ken Griffey Jr. (1991)

11. D – Brendan Ryan

12. A – True

13. B – 1984

14. A – Robinson Cano

15. C – 10

16. A – True

17. C – Kazuhiro Sasaki

18. D – Alex Rodriguez

19. B – Randy Johnson

20. A – True

DID YOU KNOW?

1. The Seattle Mariners have had two different players win American League Cy Young Awards in franchise history: Randy Johnson (1995) and Felix Hernandez (2010).

2. The Seattle Mariners have had six different players win Silver Slugger Awards in franchise history: Ken Griffey Jr. (1991, 1993, 1994, 1996, 1997, 1998, 1999), Edgar Martinez (1992, 1995, 1997, 2001, 2003), Alex Rodriguez (1996, 1998, 1999, 2000), Bret Boone (2001, 2003), Ichiro Suzuki (2007, 2009), and Nelson Cruz (2017).

3. The Seattle Mariners have four different players who have been named American League Rookie of the Year in franchise history: Alvin Davis (1984), Kazuhiro Sasaki (2000), Ichiro Suzuki (2001), and Kyle Lewis (2020).

4. The Seattle Mariners have had 14 different players win American League Gold Glove Awards in franchise history: Mark Langston, Harold Reynolds, Ken Griffey Jr., Omar Vizquel, Jay Buhner, John Olerud, Mike Cameron, Ichiro Suzuki, Bret Boone, Adrian Beltre, Franklin Gutierrez, Kyle Seager, Evan White, and J.P. Crawford.

5. The Seattle Mariners have had two different players win the American League MVP Award in franchise history: Ken Griffey Jr. (1997) and Ichiro Suzuki (2001).

6. The Seattle Mariners have had two different players win the American League Reliever of the Year Award in franchise history: J.J. Putz (2007) and Edwin Diaz (2018).

7. The Seattle Mariners have had three different players win the MLB All-Star Game MVP Award in franchise history: Ken Griffey Jr. (1992), Ichiro Suzuki (2007), and Robinson Cano (2017).

8. The Seattle Mariners have had three different players win the Wilson Defensive Player of the Year Award in franchise history: Brendan Ryan (2012), Dustin Ackley (2013), and Mike Zunino (2018).

9. Ken Griffey Jr. was named the Players Choice Awards Player of the Decade in 1999.

10. The Seattle Mariners have had three different players win the Roberto Clemente Award in franchise history: Harold Reynolds (1991), Jamie Moyer (2003), and Edgar Martinez (2004).

CHAPTER 16:

EMERALD CITY

QUIZ TIME!

1. What is the name of Seattle's famous observation tower located at the Seattle Center?

    a. Stratosphere Tower
    b. Tower of the Americas
    c. Space Needle
    d. Reunion Tower

2. Seattle is home to the world's first Starbucks store in Pike Place Market.

    a. True
    b. False

3. People in Seattle buy more per capita, of which product, than any other US city?

    a. Umbrellas
    b. Fish
    c. Coffee
    d. Sunglasses

4. Which musician is NOT from Seattle?

   a. Macklemore
   b. Mariah Carey
   c. Kenny G
   d. Sir Mix a Lot

5. Which actor from *The Office* is from Seattle?

   a. John Krasinksi (Jim)
   b. Steve Carell (Michael)
   c. Rainn Wilson (Dwight)
   d. Jenna Fischer (Pam)

6. Which company was founded in Seattle?

   a. Apple
   b. Boeing
   c. Coca Cola
   d. None of the above

7. Seattle was the first major American city to have a female mayor.

   a. True
   b. False

8. What is the name of the famous movie starring Tom Hanks and Meg Ryan, set in Seattle?

   a. *An Officer and a Gentleman*
   b. *10 Things I Hate About You*
   c. *You've Got Mail*
   d. *Sleepless in Seattle*

9. What is the name of Seattle's NFL team?

    a. Seattle 49ers
    b. Seattle Sea Dogs
    c. Seattle Seahawks
    d. Seattle Raiders

10. What is the name of Seattle's former NBA team?

    a. Seattle Kings
    b. Seattle SuperSonics
    c. Seattle Warriors
    d. Seattle Thuder

11. What is the name of the Seahawks' current stadium?

    a. Lumen Field
    b. Paul Brown Stadium
    c. Arrowhead Stadium
    d. State Farm Stadium

12. Seattle has a WNBA team called the Seattle Storm.

    a. True
    b. False

13. What is the name of the brand-new NHL team in Seattle?

    a. Seattle Sharks
    b. Seattle Golden Knights
    c. Seattle Metropolitans
    d. Seattle Kraken

14. What is the name of Seattle's MLS team?

    a. Seattle Dynamo
    b. Seattle Earthquakes

c. Seattle Sounders

d. Seattle Rapids

15. The largest man-made island in the United States is which island in Seattle?

    a. Whidbey Island

    b. Shaw Island

    c. Blake Island

    d. Harbor Island

16. Seattle's Pier 52 is the busiest ferry terminal in the United States.

    a. True

    b. False

17. What is the name of the largest public park in Seattle that consists of 11.81 miles of walking trails?

    a. Seward Park

    b. Carkeek Park

    c. Green Lake Park

    d. Discovery Park

18. What is Seattle-Tacoma International Airport's code?

    a. STA

    b. SEA

    c. SET

    d. TAC

19. More people get to work in Seattle using which method than any other city in the United States?

a. Bike

b. Walk

c. Drive

d. Skateboard

20. Seattle is the rainiest city in the United States.

a. True

b. False

QUIZ ANSWERS

1. C – Space Needle

2. A – True

3. D – Sunglasses

4. B – Mariah Carey

5. C – Rainn Wilson (Dwight)

6. B – Boeing

7. A – True

8. D – *Sleepless in Seattle*

9. C – Seattle Seahawks

10. B – Seattle SuperSonics

11. A – Lumen Field

12. A – True

13. D – Seattle Kraken

14. C – Seattle Sounders

15. D – Harbor Island

16. A – True

17. D – Discovery Park

18. B – SEA

19. A – Bike

20. B – False

DID YOU KNOW?

1. Seattle is ranked as the most literate city in the United States. They have the highest percentage of residents with a college degree as well.

2. The Seattle Public Library system has the highest percentage of library card holders in the United States.

3. Seattle's Pacific Northwest Ballet Company has the highest attendance per capita in the United States. Seattle has the second most live performances in the United States, after New York City.

4. Online retailer juggernaut Amazon was founded in Seattle in 1994.

5. Seattle is home to America's very first gas station.

6. Seattle has the largest houseboat population in the United States. In fact, the houseboat from *Sleepless in Seattle* sold for over $2 million.

7. Seattle City Light is a utility company in Seattle that powers 90% of the city via hydroelectricity, which has zero carbon footprint. The city aims to be carbon neutral by the year 2050.

8. Seattle is home to Nintendo of America and Microsoft Game Studios. Pokémon headquarters is also nearby. Seattle is incredibly important to the video game industry.

9. The Evergreen Point Floating Bridge is the longest floating bridge in the world, measuring 15,580 feet long.

10. Pike Place Market is one of the oldest farmers markets in the United States. Pike Place gets an average of 10 million visitors annually. It is the 33rd most visited tourist attraction in the world.

CHAPTER 17:

BIG UNIT

QUIZ TIME!

1. What is Randy Johnson's full name?

    a. Joseph Randall Johnson

    b. Randall Joseph Johnson

    c. Randall David Johnson

    d. David Randall Johnson

2. Randy Johnson played his entire 22-season MLB career with the Seattle Mariners.

    a. True

    b. False

3. Where was Randy Johnson born?

    a. Sacramento, California

    b. Walnut Creek, California

    c. Phoenix, Arizona

    d. Tucson, Arizona

4. When was Randy Johnson born?

a. March 10, 1960

b. March 10, 1963

c. September 10, 1960

d. September 10, 1963

5. Randy Johnson won a pitching Triple Crown in 2002.

   a. True

   b. False

6. How many Cy Young Awards did Randy Johnson win during his MLB career?

   a. 2

   b. 3

   c. 5

   d. 7

7. What year was Randy Johnson inducted into the National Baseball Hall of Fame with 97.3% of the vote?

   a. 2013

   b. 2014

   c. 2015

   d. 2016

8. Randy Johnson was named the 2001 World Series MVP.

   a. True

   b. False

9. How many World Series championships did Randy Johnson win during his MLB career?

   a. 0

   b. 1

c. 2

d. 3

10. What year did Randy Johnson make his MLB debut?

   a. 1985

   b. 1986

   c. 1987

   d. 1988

11. How many MLB All-Star Games was Randy Johnson named to during his MLB career?

   a. 6

   b. 8

   c. 10

   d. 12

12. Randy Johnson's uniform number 51 is retired by the Seattle Mariners.

   a. True

   b. False

13. Randy Johnson was inducted into the Seattle Mariners Hall of Fame in what year?

   a. 2011

   b. 2012

   c. 2013

   d. 2014

14. Randy Johnson recorded 4,875 strikeouts during his MLB career.

a. True

b. False

15. How many times did Randy Johnson win the ERA Title during his MLB career?

    a. 1

    b. 2

    c. 3

    d. 4

16. What is Randy Johnson's career ERA?

    a. 3.09

    b. 3.19

    c. 3.29

    d. 3.39

17. On May 18, 2004, Randy Johnson at age 40 became the oldest pitcher in MLB history to throw a perfect game.

    a. True

    b. False

18. How many wins did Randy Johnson record during his MLB career?

    a. 301

    b. 302

    c. 303

    d. 304

19. How many losses did Randy Johnson record during his MLB career?

a. 155

b. 166

c. 177

d. 188

20. Randy Johnson attended college at USC.

a. True

b. False

QUIZ ANSWERS

1. C – Randall David Johnson

2. B – False (He played for the Mariners, Diamondbacks, Expos, Yankees, Giants, and Astros.)

3. B – Walnut Creek, California

4. D – September 10, 1963

5. A – True

6. C – 5

7. C – 2015

8. A – True

9. B – 1 (2001)

10. D – 1988

11. C – 10

12. B – False

13. B – 2012

14. A – True

15. D – 4

16. C – 3.29

17. A – True

18. C – 303

19. B – 166

20. A – True

DID YOU KNOW?

1. Randy Johnson is one of only two pitchers (the other being Greg Maddux) to win the Cy Young Award in four consecutive seasons (1999 to 2002). In 1999, he joined Pedro Martínez and Gaylord Perry in the rare feat of winning the Cy Young Award in both the American and National Leagues.

2. Randy Johnson is one of 18 pitchers in MLB history to record a win against all 30 MLB franchises.

3. In 1982, as a senior, Randy Johnson struck out 121 batters in 66 innings, and threw a perfect game in his last high school start.

4. Randy Johnson guest starred in *The Simpsons* episode "Bart Has Two Mommies," which aired on March 19, 2006.

5. For most of his MLB career, Randy Johnson held the title of tallest player in MLB history at 6 feet 10 inches tall.

6. During Spring Training on March 24, 2001, Randy Johnson hit a dove with a fastball. Seriously, go watch it on YouTube.

7. Randy Johnson is the first member of the National Baseball Hall of Fame to be depicted in an Arizona Diamondbacks uniform on his plaque.

8. On May 8, 2001, Randy Johnson struck out 20 batters in a single game, against the Cincinnati Reds.

9. While attending USC, Randy Johnson played baseball (alongside his teammate, Mark McGwire) as well as basketball.

10. Since retiring from the MLB, Randy Johnson has pursued a second career as a photographer.

CHAPTER 18:

GAR

QUIZ TIME!

1. Where was Edgar Martinez born?

    a. Syracuse, New York

    b. Utica, New York

    c. New York, New York

    d. Buffalo, New York

2. Edgar Martinez played his entire 18-season MLB career with the Seattle Mariners.

    a. True

    b. False

3. How many Silver Slugger Awards did Edgar Martinez win during his MLB career?

    a. 1

    b. 2

    c. 3

    d. 5

4. How many Gold Glove Awards did Edgar Martinez win during his MLB career?

   a. 0
   b. 1
   c. 2
   d. 3

5. How many MLB All-Star Games was Edgar Martinez named to during his MLB career?

   a. 3
   b. 4
   c. 7
   d. 10

6. What year was Edgar Martinez inducted into the National Baseball Hall of Fame?

   a. 2016
   b. 2017
   c. 2018
   d. 2019

7. Edgar Martinez made his MLB debut in 1987.

   a. True
   b. False

8. What year did the Seattle Mariners retire Edgar Martinez's uniform number 11?

   a. 2016
   b. 2017
   c. 2018
   d. 2019

9. What year was Edgar Martinez inducted into the Seattle Mariners Hall of Fame?

    a. 2005
    b. 2006
    c. 2007
    d. 2008

10. How many times did Edgar Martinez win the American League batting title?

    a. 0
    b. 1
    c. 2
    d. 3

11. What is Edgar Martinez's career batting average?

    a. .302
    b. .312
    c. .322
    d. .323

12. Edgar Martinez served as the Seattle Mariners' hitting coach from 2015 to 2018.

    a. True
    b. False

13. How many home runs did Edgar Martinez hit during his MLB career?

    a. 109
    b. 209
    c. 309
    d. 409

14. How many RBIs did Edgar Martinez collect during his MLB career?

   a. 1,161
   b. 1,261
   c. 1,361
   d. 1,461

15. How many hits did Edgar Martinez collect during his MLB career?

   a. 1,947
   b. 2,047
   c. 2,147
   d. 2,247

16. Edgar Martinez collected 49 stolen bases during his MLB career.

   a. True
   b. False

17. Over the course of his MLB career, how many times was Edgar Martinez named the MLB Player of the Month?

   a. 2
   b. 3
   c. 4
   d. 5

18. Over the course of his MLB career, how many times was Edgar Martinez named the MLB Player of the Week?

   a. 3
   b. 5

c. 7

d. 8

19. Edgar Martinez won the Roberto Clemente Award in which year?

    a. 2001

    b. 2002

    c. 2003

    d. 2004

20. Edgar Martinez is one of 18 MLB players to record a batting average of .300, an on-base percentage of .400, and a slugging percentage of .500 in 5,000 or more plate appearances.

    a. True

    b. False

QUIZ ANSWERS

1. C – New York, New York

2. A – True

3. D – 5

4. A – 0

5. C – 7

6. D – 2019

7. A – True

8. B – 2017

9. C – 2007

10. C – 2 (1992, 1995)

11. B – .312

12. A – True

13. C – 309

14. B – 1,261

15. D – 2,247

16. A – True

17. D – 5

18. C – 7

19. D – 2004

20. A – True

DID YOU KNOW?

1. In the 1995 American League Division Series, Edgar Martinez hit "The Double." This play won the series and increased support for Mariners baseball as they attempted to fund a new stadium.

2. Edgar Martinez was the American League RBI leader in 2000.

3. Edgar Martinez was inducted into the National Baseball Hall of Fame in 2019 on his 10th ballot with 85.4% of the vote.

4. Before he signed as a free agent with the Seattle Mariners, Edgar Martinez played semi-professional baseball in Puerto Rico. He also worked as a supervisor in a furniture store during the day and in a General Electric factory overnight.

5. Edgar Martinez changed roles from hitting coach to a hitting advisor for the Seattle Mariners organization after the 2018 season in order to be able to spend more time with his family.

6. Edgar Martinez is one of the founders of Plaza Bank, Washington's first Hispanic bank. It was founded in 2005.

7. Edgar Martinez helps run Branded Solutions by Edgar Martinez, his family's embroidery business, in Tacoma, Washington.

8. In 2007, Edgar Martinez was inducted into the World Sports Humanitarian Hall of Fame, which is located in Boise, Idaho.

9. The Seattle Mariners worked with Edgar Martinez, chef Ethan Stowell, and bartender Anu Apte to create Edgar's Cantina, located at Safeco Field. Edgar's Cantina opened during the 2013 MLB season.

10. Edgar Martinez's cousin, Carmelo Martinez, played in the MLB from 1983 to 1991 with the San Diego Padres, Pittsburgh Pirates, Kansas City Royals, Cincinnati Reds, Chicago Cubs, and Philadelphia Phillies.

CONCLUSION

Now you truly are the ultimate Mariners fan! Not only did you learn about the M's of the modern era, but you also expanded your knowledge back to the early days of the franchise. We hope you learned something new about your favorite MLB franchise!

You read and answered questions about the Mariners' origins and their history. You learned about the history of their uniforms and jersey numbers, and you also read some of the craziest nicknames of all time. You learned more about the legendary Ken Griffey Jr. You also learned about the Hall-of-Famers Randy Johnson and Edgar Martinez, as well as international superstar Ichiro Suzuki.

You were amazed by Mariners stats and recalled some of the most infamous Mariners trades and draft picks of all time. You broke down your knowledge by outfielders, infielders, pitchers, and catchers. You looked back on the Mariners' playoff feats and the awards that came before, during, and after them. You also learned about the Mariners' fiercest rivalries inside and outside of their division.

Every team in the MLB has a storied history, but the Mariners have one of the most memorable of all. They have battled each and every season with the backing of their devoted fans. Being the ultimate Mariners fan takes knowledge and a whole lot of patience, which you tested with this book. Whether you knew every answer or were stumped by several questions, you learned some of the most interesting history that the game of baseball has to offer.

The deep history of the Seattle Mariners franchise represents what we all love about the game of baseball. The heart, the determination, the tough times, and the unexpected moments. Plus, the players that inspire us and encourage us to do our best, because even if you get knocked down, there is always another game and another day.

With players like Kyle Seager, Marco Gonzales, and Kyle Lewis, the future for the Mariners continues to look bright. They have a lot to prove, but there is no doubt that this franchise will continue to be one of the most competitive teams in Major League Baseball year after year.

It's a new decade, which means there is a clean slate, ready to continue writing the history of the Seattle Mariners. The ultimate M's fan cannot wait to see what's to come for their beloved boys in blue.

Made in United States
Troutdale, OR
06/06/2023